50 Savoring Spain Dishes for Home

By: Kelly Johnson

Table of Contents

- Paella Valenciana
- Tortilla Española (Spanish Omelette)
- Gazpacho
- Patatas Bravas
- Croquetas de Jamón (Ham Croquettes)
- Pisto (Spanish Ratatouille)
- Fabada Asturiana (Asturian Bean Stew)
- Salmorejo
- Albóndigas (Meatballs in Tomato Sauce)
- Pulpo a la Gallega (Galician Style Octopus)
- Churros con Chocolate
- Calamares a la Romana (Fried Squid)
- Jamón Ibérico
- Empanadas
- Tinto de Verano (Summer Wine Cocktail)
- Bacalao a la Vizcaína (Basque Style Salted Cod)
- Cochinillo Asado (Roast Suckling Pig)
- Ensalada Rusa (Russian Salad)
- Chistorra (Spanish Sausage)
- Tarta de Santiago (Almond Cake)
- Pinchos Morunos (Moorish Skewers)
- Tortilla de Patatas con Cebolla (Spanish Omelette with Onion)
- Arroz a la Cubana
- Paella de Mariscos (Seafood Paella)
- Ceviche de Gambas (Shrimp Ceviche)
- Lechazo Asado (Roast Lamb)
- Bocadillo de Calamares (Squid Sandwich)
- Cazuela de Mariscos (Seafood Casserole)
- Sopa de Ajo (Garlic Soup)
- Hígado de Pato (Duck Liver)
- Migas
- Churros con Chocolate
- Serrano Ham with Melon
- Pincho de Tortilla (Mini Spanish Omelette)
- Queso Manchego

- Piquillos Rellenos de Marisco (Piquillo Peppers Stuffed with Seafood)
- Empanadillas de Atún (Tuna Empanadas)
- Arroz Negro (Black Rice with Squid Ink)
- Morcilla (Blood Sausage)
- Sardinas a la Plancha (Grilled Sardines)
- Papas a la Riojana (Potatoes with Chorizo)
- Fideuà (Noodle Paella)
- Cordero a la Pastora (Shepherd's Lamb)
- Tarta de Queso (Spanish Cheesecake)
- Almejas a la Marinera (Clams in White Wine Sauce)
- Percebes (Gooseneck Barnacles)
- Piquillos Rellenos de Bacalao (Piquillo Peppers Stuffed with Salted Cod)
- Revuelto de Setas (Scrambled Eggs with Mushrooms)
- Sangría
- Paté de Hígado de Pato (Duck Liver Pâté)

Paella Valenciana

Ingredients:

- 1/4 cup olive oil
- 1 onion, chopped
- 2 cloves garlic, minced
- 1 bell pepper, chopped
- 2 tomatoes, peeled and chopped
- 1 1/2 cups short-grain rice (such as Arborio or Bomba)
- 4 cups chicken broth
- 1/2 teaspoon saffron threads
- 1 teaspoon paprika
- 1/2 teaspoon turmeric (optional, for color)
- 1 cup green beans, cut into 1-inch pieces
- 1/2 cup peas
- 1 lb chicken thighs or breasts, cut into chunks
- 1/2 lb rabbit (optional), cut into pieces
- 1/2 lb shrimp, peeled and deveined
- 1/2 lb mussels or clams, scrubbed
- 1/2 lb squid, cut into rings
- Salt and pepper, to taste
- Fresh parsley, for garnish
- Lemon wedges, for serving

Instructions:

1. **Prepare the Broth**:
   In a small saucepan, heat the chicken broth and infuse the saffron threads in it for about 10 minutes. Keep warm.
2. **Cook the Meat**:
   In a large paella pan, heat the olive oil over medium heat. Add the chicken and rabbit pieces (if using), and cook until browned. Remove and set aside.
3. **Cook Vegetables**:
   In the same pan, add the onion, garlic, and bell pepper. Cook for about 5 minutes until softened. Add the tomatoes and cook for an additional 5 minutes until the tomatoes break down.
4. **Add Rice and Spices**:
   Stir in the rice, paprika, and turmeric (if using), then add the infused saffron broth. Stir well, making sure the rice is coated with the oil and spices.
5. **Simmer**:
   Add the cooked chicken and rabbit back into the pan, followed by the green beans, peas, and any additional water or broth if necessary. Let everything simmer for about 10-15 minutes.

6. **Add Seafood**:
Arrange the shrimp, mussels, and squid on top of the rice. Continue to cook without stirring for an additional 10-15 minutes until the rice is cooked and the seafood is fully cooked.
7. **Serve**:
Remove from heat and let rest for 5 minutes. Garnish with fresh parsley and lemon wedges. Serve hot!

Tortilla Española (Spanish Omelette)

Ingredients:

- 1/4 cup olive oil
- 5 medium potatoes, peeled and thinly sliced
- 1 onion, thinly sliced
- 6 large eggs
- Salt and pepper, to taste

Instructions:

1. **Cook the Potatoes and Onion:**
   Heat the olive oil in a large skillet over medium heat. Add the sliced potatoes and onions, and cook, turning occasionally, until softened but not browned (about 20 minutes). Remove from heat and drain any excess oil.
2. **Whisk the Eggs:**
   In a bowl, whisk the eggs, and season with salt and pepper.
3. **Combine:**
   Add the cooked potatoes and onions into the beaten eggs and let them sit for 5-10 minutes to absorb the flavors.
4. **Cook the Omelette:**
   In the same skillet, heat a little oil over medium-low heat. Pour the egg mixture into the pan and cook slowly, shaking the pan occasionally. When the edges start to set, use a spatula to gently lift them.
5. **Flip the Tortilla:**
   Once the bottom is golden and set, cover the skillet with a plate, flip the tortilla onto the plate, and slide it back into the pan to cook the other side for another 3-4 minutes.
6. **Serve:**
   Let the tortilla rest for a few minutes before slicing and serving.

Gazpacho

Ingredients:

- 6 ripe tomatoes, chopped
- 1 cucumber, peeled and chopped
- 1 bell pepper, chopped
- 1/2 red onion, chopped
- 2 cloves garlic, minced
- 1/4 cup olive oil
- 2 tablespoons red wine vinegar
- 1 slice stale bread, soaked in water (optional)
- Salt and pepper, to taste

Instructions:

1. **Blend the Vegetables:**
   In a blender, combine the tomatoes, cucumber, bell pepper, onion, garlic, olive oil, and red wine vinegar. If using, add the soaked bread for texture.
2. **Season and Chill:**
   Blend until smooth. Season with salt and pepper to taste. Refrigerate for at least 2 hours before serving to allow the flavors to meld.
3. **Serve:**
   Serve chilled, garnished with extra chopped vegetables or a drizzle of olive oil.

Patatas Bravas

Ingredients:

- 4 large potatoes, peeled and cut into cubes
- 1/4 cup olive oil
- Salt, to taste
- For the sauce:
    - 1/2 cup tomato sauce
    - 1 teaspoon paprika
    - 1/2 teaspoon cayenne pepper
    - 1 tablespoon vinegar
    - 2 cloves garlic, minced

Instructions:

1. **Fry the Potatoes**:
   Heat the olive oil in a large frying pan over medium heat. Fry the potato cubes until golden and crispy. Remove from oil and drain on paper towels. Season with salt.
2. **Make the Sauce**:
   In a separate pan, combine the tomato sauce, paprika, cayenne pepper, vinegar, and garlic. Simmer for 5-10 minutes until thickened and fragrant.
3. **Serve**:
   Pour the sauce over the crispy potatoes and serve hot as a tapa.

Croquetas de Jamón (Ham Croquettes)

Ingredients:

- 2 tablespoons butter
- 1/2 cup flour
- 2 cups milk
- 1/2 teaspoon nutmeg
- Salt and pepper, to taste
- 1/2 cup chopped jamón serrano or ham
- 2 tablespoons chopped parsley
- 1 cup breadcrumbs
- 2 eggs, beaten
- Vegetable oil, for frying

Instructions:

1. **Make the Bechamel**:
   In a saucepan, melt the butter over medium heat. Add the flour and cook, stirring constantly, for 2-3 minutes. Gradually add the milk while stirring, creating a smooth sauce. Season with nutmeg, salt, and pepper.
2. **Add the Ham**:
   Stir in the chopped ham and parsley. Cook for another 2 minutes, then let the mixture cool in the refrigerator for at least 2 hours.
3. **Form and Coat**:
   Once the mixture is chilled, roll it into small balls or cylinders. Dip each croquette into the beaten egg and coat with breadcrumbs.
4. **Fry**:
   Heat vegetable oil in a pan over medium-high heat. Fry the croquettes until golden brown, about 3-4 minutes. Drain on paper towels.
5. **Serve**:
   Serve the croquetas warm as a tapa or appetizer.

Pisto (Spanish Ratatouille)

Ingredients:

- 1/4 cup olive oil
- 1 onion, chopped
- 1 bell pepper, chopped
- 1 zucchini, chopped
- 1 eggplant, chopped
- 3 tomatoes, chopped
- 1 teaspoon smoked paprika
- Salt and pepper, to taste
- Fresh basil, for garnish

Instructions:

1. **Cook the Vegetables**:
   In a large skillet, heat the olive oil over medium heat. Add the onion and bell pepper and sauté for 5 minutes. Add the zucchini and eggplant, and cook for an additional 10 minutes until tender.
2. **Add Tomatoes**:
   Stir in the tomatoes and paprika. Simmer for 10-15 minutes until the vegetables are soft and the flavors meld together. Season with salt and pepper.
3. **Serve**:
   Garnish with fresh basil and serve warm with crusty bread.

Fabada Asturiana (Asturian Bean Stew)

Ingredients:

- 2 cups dried white beans (such as fabes)
- 1/2 lb chorizo, sliced
- 1/2 lb morcilla (blood sausage), sliced (optional)
- 1 onion, chopped
- 2 cloves garlic, minced
- 1 bay leaf
- 1/2 teaspoon paprika
- Salt and pepper, to taste

Instructions:

1. **Soak the Beans**:
   Soak the dried beans overnight in water.
2. **Cook the Stew**:
   In a large pot, heat some oil and sauté the onion and garlic until soft. Add the chorizo, morcilla (if using), and paprika, and cook for 5 minutes.
3. **Simmer**:
   Add the soaked beans, bay leaf, and enough water to cover everything. Simmer for 1-2 hours until the beans are tender.
4. **Serve**:
   Season with salt and pepper, and serve hot with crusty bread.

Salmorejo

Ingredients:

- 6 ripe tomatoes, chopped
- 1/4 cup olive oil
- 2 cloves garlic, minced
- 1 slice stale bread
- 1 tablespoon red wine vinegar
- Salt, to taste
- Hard-boiled eggs and jamón serrano for garnish

Instructions:

1. **Blend the Soup**:
   In a blender, combine the tomatoes, garlic, olive oil, stale bread, vinegar, and salt. Blend until smooth.
2. **Chill**:
   Refrigerate the soup for at least 2 hours.
3. **Serve**:
   Serve cold, garnished with chopped hard-boiled eggs and jamón serrano.

Albóndigas (Meatballs in Tomato Sauce)

Ingredients:

- 1 lb ground beef or pork
- 1/4 cup breadcrumbs
- 1 egg
- 1/4 cup chopped parsley
- 2 cloves garlic, minced
- Salt and pepper, to taste
- 1 tablespoon olive oil
- 2 cups tomato sauce
- 1 teaspoon paprika

Instructions:

1. **Make the Meatballs**:
   In a bowl, combine the ground meat, breadcrumbs, egg, parsley, garlic, salt, and pepper. Form into small meatballs.
2. **Cook the Meatballs**:
   Heat olive oil in a skillet over medium heat. Brown the meatballs on all sides, then remove and set aside.
3. **Make the Sauce**:
   In the same pan, add the tomato sauce and paprika. Bring to a simmer, then add the meatballs back into the sauce. Simmer for 20 minutes.
4. **Serve**:
   Serve the meatballs hot with crusty bread.

Pulpo a la Gallega (Galician Style Octopus)

Ingredients:

- 2 lb octopus, cleaned
- 1 onion
- 4 cloves garlic, peeled
- 1/4 cup olive oil
- 1 teaspoon smoked paprika (preferably Pimentón de la Vera)
- Sea salt, to taste
- 1/2 lemon, sliced
- Fresh parsley, chopped, for garnish

Instructions:

1. **Prepare the Octopus**:
   Bring a large pot of water to a boil. Add the onion, garlic, and lemon slices. Once boiling, add the octopus and reduce the heat to a simmer. Cook for 45-60 minutes until the octopus is tender. You can check for doneness by inserting a fork or skewer into the thickest part of a tentacle.
2. **Slice the Octopus**:
   Once tender, remove the octopus from the water and let it cool slightly. Slice the octopus into bite-sized rounds.
3. **Season**:
   Drizzle with olive oil and sprinkle with smoked paprika and sea salt to taste. Garnish with fresh parsley.
4. **Serve**:
   Serve immediately with a squeeze of lemon on the side.

Churros con Chocolate

Ingredients:

- For the Churros:
    - 1 cup water
    - 1 tablespoon sugar
    - 1/4 teaspoon salt
    - 1 cup all-purpose flour
    - 2 tablespoons vegetable oil
    - 1/4 teaspoon cinnamon (optional)
    - Vegetable oil for frying
- For the Chocolate Sauce:
    - 4 oz dark chocolate
    - 1 cup whole milk
    - 2 tablespoons sugar
    - 1/2 teaspoon vanilla extract

Instructions:

1. **Make the Churros**:
   In a saucepan, combine water, sugar, and salt. Bring to a boil. Remove from heat and stir in the flour until smooth. Add the vegetable oil and cinnamon (if using). Transfer the dough to a piping bag fitted with a star nozzle.
2. **Fry the Churros**:
   Heat vegetable oil in a frying pan to 375°F (190°C). Pipe 4-6 inch strips of dough into the hot oil, frying a few at a time. Fry for 2-3 minutes until golden brown and crispy. Remove and drain on paper towels.
3. **Make the Chocolate Sauce**:
   In a small saucepan, heat the milk and sugar over medium heat until warm. Add the dark chocolate and stir until melted and smooth. Stir in vanilla extract.
4. **Serve**:
   Serve the churros with the chocolate sauce for dipping.

Calamares a la Romana (Fried Squid)

Ingredients:

- 1 lb squid, cleaned and cut into rings
- 1 cup flour
- 1 teaspoon paprika
- Salt and pepper, to taste
- 1 egg, beaten
- 1 cup breadcrumbs
- Vegetable oil, for frying
- Lemon wedges, for serving

Instructions:

1. **Prepare the Squid**:
   In a bowl, combine flour, paprika, salt, and pepper. Dip the squid rings first in the flour mixture, then in the beaten egg, and finally coat in breadcrumbs.
2. **Fry the Squid**:
   Heat vegetable oil in a frying pan over medium heat. Fry the squid rings in batches for 2-3 minutes until golden brown and crispy. Remove from the oil and drain on paper towels.
3. **Serve**:
   Serve the fried squid with lemon wedges and enjoy.

Jamón Ibérico

Ingredients:

- 1 lb Jamón Ibérico (Spanish cured ham), thinly sliced

Instructions:

1. **Serve**:
   Simply lay the thinly sliced Jamón Ibérico on a plate and serve as part of a Spanish tapas spread. It can be enjoyed with bread or paired with wine.

Empanadas

Ingredients:

- For the Filling:
    - 1 lb ground beef or chicken
    - 1 onion, chopped
    - 1 bell pepper, chopped
    - 1/2 cup tomato sauce
    - 1 teaspoon paprika
    - 1 teaspoon cumin
    - Salt and pepper, to taste
    - 1/2 cup olives, chopped (optional)
    - 1 boiled egg, chopped (optional)
- For the Dough:
    - 2 cups all-purpose flour
    - 1/2 teaspoon salt
    - 1/2 cup butter, cold and diced
    - 1 egg, beaten
    - 1/4 cup cold water

Instructions:

1. **Make the Filling**:
   In a skillet, cook the ground meat over medium heat until browned. Add the chopped onion, bell pepper, and cook until softened. Stir in tomato sauce, paprika, cumin, salt, and pepper. Cook for another 5 minutes. Add chopped olives and boiled egg if desired. Remove from heat and let cool.
2. **Make the Dough**:
   In a large bowl, combine the flour and salt. Cut in the butter until the mixture resembles breadcrumbs. Add the beaten egg and cold water to form a dough. Knead until smooth, then divide into small balls and roll out into circles.
3. **Assemble the Empanadas**:
   Place a spoonful of the filling in the center of each dough circle. Fold the dough over the filling to create a half-moon shape. Press the edges to seal, then crimp with a fork.
4. **Bake**:
   Preheat the oven to 375°F (190°C). Place the empanadas on a baking sheet and brush with egg wash. Bake for 25-30 minutes or until golden brown.

Tinto de Verano (Summer Wine Cocktail)

Ingredients:

- 3 parts red wine (preferably Spanish)
- 1 part lemon soda (or sparkling water)
- Ice cubes
- Lemon slices, for garnish

Instructions:

1. **Mix**:
   In a glass, combine the red wine and lemon soda. Stir gently.
2. **Serve**:
   Fill the glass with ice cubes and garnish with lemon slices. Serve chilled.

Bacalao a la Vizcaína (Basque Style Salted Cod)

Ingredients:

- 1 lb salted cod, soaked and desalted
- 1 onion, chopped
- 2 cloves garlic, minced
- 1/4 cup olive oil
- 2 tomatoes, peeled and chopped
- 1/2 teaspoon smoked paprika
- 1/4 cup red wine
- Salt and pepper, to taste
- Fresh parsley, for garnish

Instructions:

1. **Prepare the Cod**:
   Soak the salted cod in water for 24-48 hours, changing the water every 8 hours to desalinate it.
2. **Cook the Sauce**:
   Heat olive oil in a skillet over medium heat. Add the chopped onion and garlic, and sauté until softened. Add the tomatoes, paprika, red wine, and cook for 10-15 minutes until the sauce thickens. Season with salt and pepper.
3. **Cook the Cod**:
   Add the desalted cod to the sauce and cook for 10-15 minutes, until the cod is tender and fully cooked through.
4. **Serve**:
   Garnish with fresh parsley and serve with crusty bread.

Cochinillo Asado (Roast Suckling Pig)

Ingredients:

- 1 suckling pig (around 5-7 lbs)
- 1/4 cup olive oil
- 4 cloves garlic, minced
- 1 tablespoon fresh rosemary, chopped
- 1 tablespoon fresh thyme, chopped
- Salt and pepper, to taste
- 2 cups white wine

Instructions:

1. **Prepare the Pig**:
   Preheat the oven to 400°F (200°C). Rub the suckling pig with olive oil, minced garlic, rosemary, thyme, salt, and pepper.
2. **Roast**:
   Place the pig on a roasting rack in a large roasting pan. Pour white wine into the pan and roast for 1.5 to 2 hours, basting the pig every 30 minutes with the pan juices.
3. **Serve**:
   Once the skin is crispy and golden, remove the pig from the oven. Let rest for 10 minutes before carving and serving.

Ensalada Rusa (Russian Salad)

Ingredients:

- 4 medium potatoes, peeled and cubed
- 2 carrots, peeled and chopped
- 1/2 cup peas
- 1/2 cup mayonnaise
- 1/4 cup olives, chopped
- Salt and pepper, to taste

Instructions:

1. **Boil the Vegetables**:
   Boil the potatoes and carrots in a large pot of salted water until tender, about 15 minutes. Add the peas for the last 5 minutes of cooking.
2. **Assemble the Salad**:
   Drain the vegetables and let them cool. In a large bowl, combine the potatoes, carrots, peas, mayonnaise, and chopped olives. Stir gently to combine.
3. **Serve**:
   Season with salt and pepper, and serve chilled.

Chistorra (Spanish Sausage)

Ingredients:

- 1 lb ground pork
- 1/4 cup pork fat, finely chopped
- 1/4 cup white wine
- 2 cloves garlic, minced
- 1 teaspoon paprika (preferably smoked)
- 1/2 teaspoon dried oregano
- 1/2 teaspoon ground cumin
- 1/4 teaspoon chili flakes (optional, for heat)
- Salt and pepper, to taste
- Sausage casings (optional)

Instructions:

1. **Prepare the Meat Mixture**:
   In a large bowl, combine the ground pork, pork fat, garlic, paprika, oregano, cumin, chili flakes (if using), salt, and pepper. Gradually add the white wine, mixing thoroughly until the mixture becomes smooth and well-combined.
2. **Stuff the Sausages** (optional):
   If using casings, stuff the sausage mixture into the casings, twisting them into 6-inch links. Tie the ends of each link with kitchen twine. If not using casings, form the sausage mixture into small logs.
3. **Cook the Sausages**:
   Heat a little olive oil in a pan over medium heat. Cook the sausages, turning occasionally, for about 15 minutes, or until browned and cooked through.
4. **Serve**:
   Serve the chistorra with crusty bread or as a tapa.

Tarta de Santiago (Almond Cake)

Ingredients:

- 2 cups ground almonds
- 1 cup sugar
- 4 large eggs
- 1 tablespoon lemon zest
- 1/4 teaspoon cinnamon
- 1/4 teaspoon salt
- 1/4 cup all-purpose flour
- Powdered sugar, for dusting
- A stencil of the Cross of Saint James (optional, for decoration)

Instructions:

1. **Preheat the Oven**:
   Preheat your oven to 350°F (175°C). Grease and flour a round cake pan (about 9 inches in diameter).
2. **Make the Cake Batter**:
   In a large bowl, whisk together the ground almonds, sugar, eggs, lemon zest, cinnamon, salt, and flour. Mix until smooth.
3. **Bake the Cake**:
   Pour the batter into the prepared cake pan and bake for 30-35 minutes, or until the cake is set and a toothpick comes out clean.
4. **Serve**:
   Once cooled, dust the cake with powdered sugar. If desired, place a stencil of the Cross of Saint James on top before dusting for the traditional decoration.

Pinchos Morunos (Moorish Skewers)

Ingredients:

- 1 lb boneless pork shoulder or chicken, cut into cubes
- 2 tablespoons olive oil
- 2 teaspoons ground cumin
- 1 teaspoon paprika
- 1/2 teaspoon ground cinnamon
- 1 teaspoon garlic powder
- 1 tablespoon white wine vinegar
- Salt and pepper, to taste
- Fresh parsley, chopped, for garnish

Instructions:

1. **Marinate the Meat**:
   In a bowl, mix the olive oil, cumin, paprika, cinnamon, garlic powder, vinegar, salt, and pepper. Add the cubed pork or chicken, toss to coat, and let marinate for at least 30 minutes.
2. **Skewer and Cook**:
   Thread the marinated meat onto skewers. Preheat a grill or grill pan over medium-high heat. Grill the skewers for about 6-8 minutes per side, until the meat is cooked through.
3. **Serve**:
   Garnish with fresh parsley and serve with a side of bread or a salad.

Tortilla de Patatas con Cebolla (Spanish Omelette with Onion)

Ingredients:

- 4 large potatoes, peeled and thinly sliced
- 1 onion, thinly sliced
- 6 large eggs
- 1/4 cup olive oil
- Salt and pepper, to taste

Instructions:

1. **Cook the Potatoes and Onions**:
   Heat the olive oil in a large frying pan over medium heat. Add the sliced potatoes and onions, and cook for 20-25 minutes, stirring occasionally, until soft and golden brown. Season with salt and pepper.
2. **Prepare the Eggs**:
   In a separate bowl, beat the eggs and season with salt and pepper. Once the potatoes and onions are cooked, drain any excess oil and add the mixture to the eggs. Stir to combine.
3. **Cook the Tortilla**:
   Return the mixture to the frying pan and cook over low heat. Once the edges start to set, use a spatula to gently lift the sides, allowing uncooked egg to flow underneath. When the tortilla is mostly set but still a little runny on top, carefully flip it using a plate and cook the other side for 3-4 minutes.
4. **Serve**:
   Serve the tortilla warm or at room temperature, cut into wedges.

Arroz a la Cubana

Ingredients:

- 2 cups long-grain white rice
- 4 eggs
- 1/2 cup tomato sauce
- 2 tablespoons olive oil
- 1/4 teaspoon garlic powder
- Salt, to taste
- 1/4 cup frozen peas (optional)
- Plantains or bananas (optional, for garnish)

Instructions:

1. **Cook the Rice**:
   Cook the rice according to package instructions. If desired, add frozen peas during the last few minutes of cooking.
2. **Fry the Eggs**:
   Heat olive oil in a pan over medium heat and fry the eggs to your liking (traditionally sunny-side-up).
3. **Serve**:
   Serve the rice with a fried egg on top. Spoon tomato sauce over the rice and garnish with fried plantains or sliced bananas if desired.

Paella de Mariscos (Seafood Paella)

Ingredients:

- 2 tablespoons olive oil
- 1 onion, chopped
- 2 cloves garlic, minced
- 1 bell pepper, chopped
- 2 tomatoes, chopped
- 1 1/2 cups short-grain rice (such as Arborio)
- 4 cups seafood stock or chicken broth
- 1/2 teaspoon saffron threads (optional)
- 1/2 teaspoon paprika
- 1 lb mixed seafood (shrimp, mussels, clams, squid)
- 1/4 cup peas
- Salt and pepper, to taste
- Lemon wedges, for garnish

Instructions:

1. **Prepare the Base**:
   Heat olive oil in a large paella pan or skillet over medium heat. Add the onion, garlic, bell pepper, and tomatoes, and sauté until softened.
2. **Cook the Rice**:
   Add the rice and stir for 1-2 minutes to coat with the vegetables. Add the seafood stock, saffron (if using), paprika, salt, and pepper. Bring to a simmer.
3. **Add the Seafood**:
   Arrange the seafood on top of the rice. Simmer for about 10-12 minutes, until the rice is cooked and the seafood is tender. Add peas during the last few minutes of cooking.
4. **Serve**:
   Serve the paella with lemon wedges on the side.

Ceviche de Gambas (Shrimp Ceviche)

Ingredients:

- 1 lb shrimp, peeled and deveined
- 1/2 red onion, thinly sliced
- 1 cucumber, peeled and diced
- 1-2 jalapeños, diced (optional)
- 1/4 cup fresh cilantro, chopped
- Juice of 3 limes
- Juice of 1 lemon
- Salt and pepper, to taste

Instructions:

1. **Cook the Shrimp**:
   Boil the shrimp for 2-3 minutes until pink and cooked through. Remove from water and let cool. Once cooled, chop into bite-sized pieces.
2. **Marinate the Shrimp**:
   In a bowl, combine the chopped shrimp, red onion, cucumber, jalapeños, and cilantro. Pour the lime and lemon juice over the mixture, and season with salt and pepper. Let it marinate in the fridge for 30 minutes.
3. **Serve**:
   Serve the ceviche chilled, garnished with more cilantro and lime wedges.

Lechazo Asado (Roast Lamb)

Ingredients:

- 4-6 lbs lamb leg or shoulder, bone-in
- 4 cloves garlic, minced
- 2 tablespoons olive oil
- 1 tablespoon rosemary, chopped
- 1 tablespoon thyme, chopped
- Salt and pepper, to taste
- 1 cup white wine

Instructions:

1. **Prepare the Lamb**:
   Preheat the oven to 400°F (200°C). Rub the lamb with garlic, olive oil, rosemary, thyme, salt, and pepper.
2. **Roast the Lamb**:
   Place the lamb in a roasting pan and pour the white wine around the meat. Roast for 1.5-2 hours, or until the meat reaches an internal temperature of 145°F (63°C) for medium-rare.
3. **Serve**:
   Let the lamb rest for 10 minutes before carving and serving.

Bocadillo de Calamares (Squid Sandwich)

Ingredients:

- 1 lb squid, cleaned and sliced into rings
- 1 cup flour
- Salt and pepper, to taste
- Vegetable oil, for frying
- 4 baguette rolls or crusty bread
- Lemon wedges, for garnish
- Aioli or mayonnaise, for spreading (optional)

Instructions:

1. **Fry the Squid**:
   Coat the squid rings in flour seasoned with salt and pepper. Heat vegetable oil in a frying pan over medium heat. Fry the squid in batches until golden and crispy, about 2-3 minutes per batch. Remove and drain on paper towels.
2. **Assemble the Sandwiches**:
   Slice the baguette rolls and spread with aioli or mayonnaise if desired. Fill with the fried squid rings.
3. **Serve**:
   Serve the squid sandwiches with lemon wedges for squeezing over the top.

Cazuela de Mariscos (Seafood Casserole)

Ingredients:

- 1 lb mixed seafood (shrimp, mussels, squid, clams)
- 1/2 lb white fish (cod or hake), cut into chunks
- 1 onion, finely chopped
- 2 cloves garlic, minced
- 1 red bell pepper, chopped
- 2 tomatoes, chopped
- 1/4 cup white wine
- 2 tablespoons olive oil
- 2 cups seafood stock
- 1 teaspoon paprika (preferably smoked)
- 1/4 teaspoon saffron threads (optional)
- Salt and pepper, to taste
- Fresh parsley, chopped, for garnish
- Lemon wedges, for serving

Instructions:

1. **Prepare the Base**:
   Heat olive oil in a large casserole dish over medium heat. Add the onion, garlic, and bell pepper, cooking until softened, about 5 minutes. Add the chopped tomatoes and cook for another 5 minutes.
2. **Add the Seafood**:
   Add the white wine, paprika, and saffron (if using). Stir, and then add the seafood stock. Bring to a simmer and cook for 10 minutes.
3. **Cook the Seafood**:
   Add the mixed seafood and fish chunks to the casserole, cooking for an additional 5-7 minutes, or until the seafood is cooked through.
4. **Serve**:
   Garnish with chopped parsley and serve with lemon wedges on the side.

Sopa de Ajo (Garlic Soup)

Ingredients:

- 8 cloves garlic, thinly sliced
- 1 onion, chopped
- 2 tablespoons olive oil
- 4 cups chicken or vegetable broth
- 1 teaspoon paprika (smoked or regular)
- 2 large eggs
- 2 slices stale bread, torn into pieces
- Salt and pepper, to taste
- Fresh parsley, chopped, for garnish

Instructions:

1. **Sauté Garlic and Onion**:
   Heat olive oil in a large pot over medium heat. Add the garlic and onion, cooking until soft and fragrant, about 5 minutes.
2. **Make the Broth**:
   Add the paprika and cook for 1 minute. Pour in the broth, bring to a simmer, and cook for 10 minutes.
3. **Add the Bread**:
   Add the torn bread to the soup, stirring to combine. Let it cook for another 5 minutes until the bread breaks down and thickens the soup.
4. **Poach the Eggs**:
   Crack the eggs into the soup, making sure to space them out. Cover and cook for 3-5 minutes until the eggs are poached to your liking.
5. **Serve**:
   Serve the soup in bowls, garnished with fresh parsley.

Hígado de Pato (Duck Liver)

Ingredients:

- 1/2 lb duck liver
- 1 tablespoon olive oil
- 1/4 cup brandy or cognac
- Salt and pepper, to taste
- Fresh thyme or rosemary, for garnish

Instructions:

1. **Cook the Liver:**
   Heat olive oil in a pan over medium-high heat. Season the duck liver with salt and pepper. Add the liver to the pan and sear for 2-3 minutes per side, until browned but still slightly pink in the center.
2. **Flambé with Brandy:**
   Carefully add the brandy or cognac to the pan and ignite with a match to flambé. Let the alcohol burn off, then simmer for another 2 minutes.
3. **Serve:**
   Serve the duck liver with fresh herbs, such as thyme or rosemary, for garnish.

Migas

Ingredients:

- 4 cups day-old bread, torn into small pieces
- 3 tablespoons olive oil
- 1 onion, chopped
- 2 cloves garlic, minced
- 1 bell pepper, chopped
- 1/2 lb chorizo, sliced
- 1/2 teaspoon paprika
- Salt and pepper, to taste
- Fresh parsley, chopped, for garnish

Instructions:

1. **Prepare the Bread:**
   In a large pan, heat the olive oil over medium heat. Add the torn bread pieces and toast them until golden brown, about 5-7 minutes.
2. **Cook the Vegetables and Chorizo:**
   In a separate pan, sauté the onion, garlic, bell pepper, and chorizo until the vegetables are softened and the chorizo is browned, about 8-10 minutes.
3. **Combine:**
   Add the cooked vegetables and chorizo to the pan with the bread. Sprinkle with paprika, salt, and pepper. Stir well to combine and cook for another 5 minutes.
4. **Serve:**
   Garnish with fresh parsley and serve warm.

Churros con Chocolate

Ingredients:

- 1 cup water
- 1/4 cup butter
- 1 cup all-purpose flour
- 1/4 teaspoon salt
- 1 teaspoon sugar
- 2 eggs
- Vegetable oil, for frying
- 1/2 cup sugar (for coating)
- 1 teaspoon cinnamon (for coating)

For the Chocolate Sauce:

- 4 oz dark chocolate
- 1/2 cup milk
- 1 tablespoon sugar

Instructions:

1. **Make the Dough**:
   In a saucepan, bring the water and butter to a boil. Once boiling, add the flour, salt, and sugar, stirring until the dough forms a ball. Remove from heat and allow to cool slightly.
2. **Shape the Churros**:
   Beat the eggs into the dough one at a time until smooth. Fill a piping bag with the dough and pipe the churros into long, thin strips.
3. **Fry the Churros**:
   Heat vegetable oil in a pan over medium heat. Fry the churros in batches for 3-4 minutes, or until golden brown and crispy.
4. **Make the Chocolate Sauce**:
   In a saucepan, melt the dark chocolate with the milk and sugar, stirring until smooth.
5. **Serve**:
   Coat the churros with cinnamon sugar and serve with the warm chocolate sauce for dipping.

Serrano Ham with Melon

Ingredients:

- 8 slices Serrano ham
- 1/2 cantaloupe or melon of choice, cut into wedges

Instructions:

1. **Prepare the Melon**:
   Cut the melon into wedges or cubes, removing the seeds.
2. **Assemble the Dish**:
   Wrap each slice of Serrano ham around a wedge of melon.
3. **Serve**:
   Serve immediately as a refreshing tapa.

Pincho de Tortilla (Mini Spanish Omelette)

Ingredients:

- 4 large eggs
- 1/2 cup potatoes, thinly sliced
- 1 small onion, chopped
- 2 tablespoons olive oil
- Salt and pepper, to taste

Instructions:

1. **Cook the Potatoes and Onion**:
   In a skillet, heat olive oil over medium heat. Add the sliced potatoes and onion, cooking until soft and golden, about 10 minutes.
2. **Make the Omelette**:
   In a bowl, whisk the eggs and season with salt and pepper. Add the cooked potatoes and onions to the eggs, mixing gently.
3. **Cook the Tortilla**:
   Heat a bit more oil in the skillet. Pour the egg mixture back into the pan, cooking over low heat until set. Flip the tortilla and cook the other side for 2-3 minutes.
4. **Serve**:
   Cut into small squares or wedges and serve as pinchos with toothpicks.

Queso Manchego

Ingredients:

- 1 wheel of Manchego cheese

Instructions:

1. **Serve the Cheese:**
   Simply slice the Manchego cheese and serve with a drizzle of olive oil or a sprinkle of dried oregano.

Piquillos Rellenos de Marisco (Piquillo Peppers Stuffed with Seafood)

Ingredients:

- 12 piquillo peppers, jarred or roasted
- 1/2 lb shrimp, cooked and chopped
- 1/4 cup crab meat (optional)
- 1/4 cup cream cheese
- 2 tablespoons mayonnaise
- 1 teaspoon paprika
- Salt and pepper, to taste
- Olive oil for drizzling

Instructions:

1. **Prepare the Filling**:
   In a bowl, combine the chopped shrimp, crab meat, cream cheese, mayonnaise, paprika, salt, and pepper.
2. **Stuff the Peppers**:
   Carefully stuff each piquillo pepper with the seafood mixture.
3. **Serve**:
   Arrange on a platter and drizzle with a little olive oil. Serve chilled or at room temperature.

Empanadillas de Atún (Tuna Empanadas)

Ingredients:

- 1 can (6 oz) tuna, drained
- 1/2 onion, finely chopped
- 1/4 cup tomato sauce
- 1 boiled egg, chopped
- 1/4 cup olives, chopped
- 1/2 teaspoon paprika
- 1 package empanada dough (store-bought or homemade)

Instructions:

1. **Make the Filling**:
   In a pan, sauté the onion in olive oil until softened. Add the tuna, tomato sauce, paprika, chopped egg, and olives. Stir well and cook for 5 minutes.
2. **Assemble the Empanadillas**:
   Place a spoonful of the tuna mixture onto each empanada dough circle. Fold over and seal the edges.
3. **Fry or Bake**:
   Fry the empanadillas in hot oil until golden, or bake in a preheated oven at 375°F (190°C) for about 20 minutes, until crispy.

Arroz Negro (Black Rice with Squid Ink)

Ingredients:

- 1 lb squid, cleaned and cut into rings
- 1 onion, finely chopped
- 2 cloves garlic, minced
- 1 red bell pepper, chopped
- 2 tomatoes, grated or blended
- 1/2 teaspoon smoked paprika
- 2 tablespoons olive oil
- 2 cups short-grain rice (like Arborio or Bomba)
- 4 cups seafood or fish stock
- 2 tablespoons squid ink
- Salt and pepper, to taste
- Fresh parsley, chopped, for garnish
- Lemon wedges, for serving

Instructions:

1. **Cook the Squid:**
   Heat olive oil in a large paella pan or skillet over medium heat. Add the chopped onion, garlic, and bell pepper, sautéing until softened, about 5 minutes. Add the squid rings and cook for 2-3 minutes until slightly golden.
2. **Make the Base:**
   Stir in the grated tomatoes and paprika, and cook for another 5 minutes. Add the rice, stirring to coat it in the tomato mixture.
3. **Add Stock and Ink:**
   Pour in the seafood stock and stir in the squid ink. Bring to a simmer and cook for 15-20 minutes, or until the rice is tender and the liquid is absorbed. If needed, add more stock as it cooks.
4. **Serve:**
   Season with salt and pepper, garnish with fresh parsley, and serve with lemon wedges on the side.

Morcilla (Blood Sausage)

Ingredients:

- 1 lb morcilla (Spanish blood sausage)
- Olive oil, for frying

Instructions:

1. **Prepare the Morcilla**:
   Slice the morcilla into 1/2-inch thick pieces.
2. **Fry the Morcilla**:
   Heat a small amount of olive oil in a pan over medium heat. Fry the morcilla slices for 3-4 minutes on each side, until crispy on the outside and cooked through.
3. **Serve**:
   Serve hot, as a tapa or alongside other dishes like potatoes or bread.

Sardinas a la Plancha (Grilled Sardines)

Ingredients:

- 12 fresh sardines, cleaned and gutted
- 2 tablespoons olive oil
- 1 clove garlic, minced
- Sea salt, to taste
- Lemon wedges, for serving
- Fresh parsley, chopped, for garnish

Instructions:

1. **Prepare the Sardines**:
   Rinse the sardines and pat them dry with paper towels. Drizzle with olive oil and rub the minced garlic over the fish. Season with sea salt.
2. **Grill the Sardines**:
   Heat a grill or grill pan over medium-high heat. Grill the sardines for 2-3 minutes per side, or until golden and crispy.
3. **Serve**:
   Garnish with fresh parsley and serve with lemon wedges for squeezing over the top.

Papas a la Riojana (Potatoes with Chorizo)

Ingredients:

- 4 large potatoes, peeled and sliced
- 1/2 lb chorizo sausage, sliced
- 1 onion, chopped
- 2 cloves garlic, minced
- 1 teaspoon smoked paprika
- 2 cups chicken or vegetable stock
- Olive oil, for frying
- Salt and pepper, to taste
- Fresh parsley, chopped, for garnish

Instructions:

1. **Cook the Chorizo**:
   In a large pot, heat olive oil over medium heat. Add the chorizo slices and cook for 5 minutes until browned. Remove and set aside.
2. **Sauté the Vegetables**:
   In the same pot, add the onion and garlic. Sauté until soft, about 5 minutes. Stir in the smoked paprika.
3. **Cook the Potatoes**:
   Add the sliced potatoes to the pot, and pour in the chicken stock. Bring to a simmer, cover, and cook for 20-25 minutes, until the potatoes are tender.
4. **Combine and Serve**:
   Add the cooked chorizo back into the pot. Stir well, season with salt and pepper, and garnish with fresh parsley.

Fideuà (Noodle Paella)

Ingredients:

- 1 lb seafood (shrimp, squid, mussels)
- 1 onion, chopped
- 1 bell pepper, chopped
- 2 cloves garlic, minced
- 2 tomatoes, grated or blended
- 1 1/2 cups fideuà noodles (or short spaghetti)
- 3 cups seafood stock
- 1 teaspoon smoked paprika
- 1/2 teaspoon saffron threads (optional)
- Olive oil, for frying
- Salt and pepper, to taste
- Fresh parsley, chopped, for garnish
- Lemon wedges, for serving

Instructions:

1. **Cook the Seafood:**
   In a large paella pan or skillet, heat olive oil over medium heat. Add the seafood and cook for 3-4 minutes until just cooked through. Remove and set aside.
2. **Prepare the Base:**
   In the same pan, add the onion, bell pepper, and garlic. Sauté until soft, about 5 minutes. Add the grated tomatoes, smoked paprika, and saffron, cooking for 5 more minutes.
3. **Cook the Noodles:**
   Add the fideuà noodles to the pan, stirring to coat in the tomato mixture. Pour in the seafood stock and bring to a boil. Lower the heat and simmer for 10-15 minutes until the noodles are tender and the liquid has been absorbed.
4. **Finish the Dish:**
   Add the seafood back to the pan, stirring gently. Season with salt and pepper, and garnish with fresh parsley.
5. **Serve:**
   Serve with lemon wedges on the side.

Cordero a la Pastora (Shepherd's Lamb)

Ingredients:

- 1 1/2 lbs lamb shoulder, cut into chunks
- 2 onions, chopped
- 2 cloves garlic, minced
- 2 tomatoes, chopped
- 1/2 cup red wine
- 1 cup chicken stock
- 2 teaspoons fresh rosemary, chopped
- 2 teaspoons paprika
- Olive oil, for frying
- Salt and pepper, to taste

Instructions:

1. **Brown the Lamb**:
   In a large pot, heat olive oil over medium-high heat. Add the lamb chunks and brown on all sides, about 5-7 minutes. Remove and set aside.
2. **Sauté the Vegetables**:
   In the same pot, add the onions and garlic. Sauté until soft, about 5 minutes. Stir in the tomatoes, rosemary, paprika, salt, and pepper. Cook for another 5 minutes.
3. **Cook the Lamb**:
   Add the wine and chicken stock to the pot, stirring to combine. Add the browned lamb back into the pot. Bring to a simmer and cook for 1-1.5 hours, until the lamb is tender and the sauce has thickened.
4. **Serve**:
   Serve hot with potatoes or crusty bread.

Tarta de Queso (Spanish Cheesecake)

Ingredients:

- 1 1/2 cups cream cheese, softened
- 1 cup heavy cream
- 3/4 cup sugar
- 1 tablespoon vanilla extract
- 3 large eggs
- 1/4 cup all-purpose flour
- 1/2 teaspoon lemon zest (optional)

Instructions:

1. **Preheat the Oven:**
   Preheat the oven to 325°F (160°C). Grease and line a springform pan with parchment paper.
2. **Make the Cheesecake Batter:**
   In a large bowl, beat the cream cheese with the sugar and vanilla extract until smooth. Add the eggs one at a time, beating after each addition. Mix in the heavy cream, flour, and lemon zest (if using), stirring until smooth.
3. **Bake the Cheesecake:**
   Pour the batter into the prepared pan. Bake for 40-50 minutes, or until the center is set but still slightly wobbly. Turn off the oven and leave the cheesecake in for 1 hour with the door slightly ajar.
4. **Chill and Serve:**
   Let the cheesecake cool to room temperature, then refrigerate for at least 4 hours before serving.

Almejas a la Marinera (Clams in White Wine Sauce)

Ingredients:

- 2 lbs fresh clams, cleaned
- 1/2 cup white wine
- 3 tablespoons olive oil
- 3 cloves garlic, minced
- 1 small onion, finely chopped
- 1/2 teaspoon smoked paprika
- 1/2 cup fresh parsley, chopped
- Salt and pepper, to taste
- Lemon wedges, for serving

Instructions:

1. **Prepare the Clams**:
   Rinse the clams thoroughly and discard any that do not close when tapped.
2. **Cook the Aromatics**:
   In a large pan, heat olive oil over medium heat. Add the onion and garlic, and sauté for about 5 minutes until softened. Add the smoked paprika and cook for 1 minute more.
3. **Add the Wine and Clams**:
   Pour in the white wine and bring it to a simmer. Add the clams to the pan and cover. Cook for 5-7 minutes, or until the clams have opened up.
4. **Finish the Dish**:
   Season with salt and pepper, then sprinkle with fresh parsley.
5. **Serve**:
   Serve the clams with the broth and lemon wedges on the side for squeezing.

Percebes (Gooseneck Barnacles)

Ingredients:

- 2 lbs fresh percebes (gooseneck barnacles)
- Sea salt, for boiling

Instructions:

1. **Boil the Percebes**:
   Bring a large pot of salted water to a boil. Add the percebes and cook for 5-7 minutes.
2. **Drain and Serve**:
   Drain the barnacles and let them cool slightly. To eat, simply twist the hard shell to remove the meat, dipping it in salt if desired.

Piquillos Rellenos de Bacalao (Piquillo Peppers Stuffed with Salted Cod)

Ingredients:

- 12 piquillo peppers, jarred or fresh
- 1 lb salted cod, soaked and shredded
- 1 onion, finely chopped
- 2 cloves garlic, minced
- 1/4 cup olive oil
- 1/2 cup milk
- 1 tablespoon flour
- Salt and pepper, to taste
- Fresh parsley, chopped, for garnish

Instructions:

1. **Prepare the Cod**:
   Soak the salted cod overnight, then shred it into pieces.
2. **Make the Filling**:
   In a pan, heat olive oil and sauté the onion and garlic until soft. Stir in the cod, and cook for 5 minutes. Add the milk and flour, and cook for another 5-7 minutes until the mixture thickens. Season with salt and pepper.
3. **Stuff the Peppers**:
   Carefully stuff each piquillo pepper with the cod mixture.
4. **Serve**:
   Garnish with fresh parsley and serve the stuffed peppers as an appetizer or tapa.

Revuelto de Setas (Scrambled Eggs with Mushrooms)

Ingredients:

- 8 large eggs
- 1 lb mushrooms, sliced (use a mix of wild mushrooms if available)
- 2 tablespoons olive oil
- 2 cloves garlic, minced
- 1/4 cup fresh parsley, chopped
- Salt and pepper, to taste

Instructions:

1. **Sauté the Mushrooms**:
   In a pan, heat olive oil over medium heat. Add the garlic and mushrooms, and sauté until the mushrooms are tender and browned, about 8 minutes.
2. **Scramble the Eggs**:
   In a bowl, beat the eggs and season with salt and pepper. Pour the eggs into the pan with the mushrooms and cook over low heat, stirring gently, until the eggs are scrambled but still creamy.
3. **Serve**:
   Sprinkle with fresh parsley and serve immediately.

Sangría

Ingredients:

- 1 bottle red wine (Spanish Rioja or Tempranillo)
- 1/4 cup brandy
- 1/4 cup orange juice
- 1/4 cup lemon juice
- 2 tablespoons sugar (optional, depending on sweetness)
- 1 orange, sliced
- 1 lemon, sliced
- 1 apple, cored and chopped
- 1 cinnamon stick
- 2 cups club soda or sparkling water
- Ice, for serving

Instructions:

1. **Mix the Sangría**:
   In a large pitcher or bowl, combine the wine, brandy, orange juice, lemon juice, and sugar (if using). Stir until the sugar dissolves.
2. **Add the Fruits and Spices**:
   Add the sliced orange, lemon, apple, and cinnamon stick. Stir well and refrigerate for at least 2-4 hours (overnight for best flavor).
3. **Serve**:
   Before serving, add the club soda or sparkling water for fizz, and pour over ice in glasses.

Paté de Hígado de Pato (Duck Liver Pâté)

Ingredients:

- 1/2 lb duck liver, cleaned
- 1/2 onion, finely chopped
- 1/4 cup brandy
- 1/4 cup heavy cream
- 1/4 cup duck fat or butter
- Salt and pepper, to taste
- Fresh thyme, for garnish
- Toasted baguette slices, for serving

Instructions:

1. **Cook the Duck Liver**:
   In a pan, heat the duck fat or butter over medium heat. Add the onion and cook until softened, about 5 minutes. Add the duck liver and cook for 3-4 minutes on each side, until browned but still slightly pink inside. Remove from the pan and set aside.
2. **Deglaze and Blend**:
   Add the brandy to the pan to deglaze, scraping up any bits from the bottom. Allow the alcohol to cook off, then add the heavy cream. Stir until the sauce thickens, about 3-4 minutes.
3. **Blend the Pâté**:
   Transfer the cooked duck liver and sauce into a food processor and blend until smooth. Season with salt and pepper.
4. **Chill and Serve**:
   Transfer the pâté to a serving dish and refrigerate for at least 2 hours to firm up. Serve with toasted baguette slices and garnish with fresh thyme.

www.ingramcontent.com/pod-product-compliance
Lightning Source LLC
LaVergne TN
LVHW081329060526
838201LV00055B/2530